Hua Mulan

ASIAPAC COMIC SERIES

Hua Mulan
China's Sweetest Magnolia

Edited & Illustrated by Xu Deyuan and Jiang Wei
Translated by Wang Jian

花木蘭

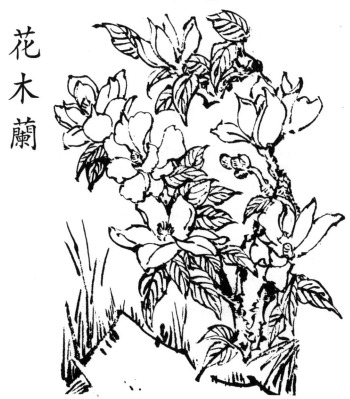

ASIAPAC • SINGAPORE

Publisher
ASIAPAC BOOKS PTE LTD
996 Bendemeer Road #06-08/09
Kallang Basin Industrial Estate
Singapore 339944
Tel: (65) 392 8455
Fax: (65) 392 6455
Email apacbks@singnet.com.sg

Visit us at our Internet home page
www.asiapacbooks.com

First published February 1996
Reprinted October 1998

©1996 ASIAPAC BOOKS, SINGAPORE
ISBN 981-3029-91-9

All rights reserved. No part of this publication may be reproduced, stored in a retrieval system, or transmitted, in any form or by any means, electronic, mechanical, photocopying, recording, or otherwise, without the prior permission of the publisher. Under no circumstances shall it be rented, resold or redistributed. If this copy is defective, kindly exchange it at the above address.

Cover design by Cheng Yew Chung
Typeset by Unistar Graphics Pte Ltd
Body text in 8/9pt Helvetica
Printed in Singapore by Loi Printing Pte Ltd

Publisher's Note

In our efforts to promote Chinese culture, we would feel regret should we fail to present through our comic series Hua Mulan, the *only* woman warrior in the history of China, or even the world, in terms of disguising herself as a man in order to join the army for her invalid father.

Whilst Hua Mulan succeeded in relieving her father of his military obligation, she had invariably put herself in the forefront of not only the battlefield but women's contention for equal capability. She unconsciously spearheaded the effort to challenge the traditional notion of male superiority in a given scenario.

Over the last hundreds of years, Hua Mulan has become an unfailing source of inspiration for many Chinese women to devote themselves to a noble and just cause.

Simple as the plot is, the spirit is abiding. The lifelike drawings depicting the moving story of this legendary figure are sure to charm you even long after you close the book.

Here we would like to express our sincere thanks to artists Xu Deyuan and Jiang Wei for the comics and the production team for their efforts in the publication of this book.

About the Illustrators

Xu Deyuan, born in August 1962 in Dalian, is a professional artist working with The Cultural Centre, Xiuyan County, Liaoning Province, the People's Republic of China. His works, including New Year's pictures, cartoons and comics, have been on display at a number of exhibitions in China and overseas and have won him a couple of prizes. He is most skilled in drawing comics.

Jiang Wei, a permanent resident of Singapore, graduated from the Affiliated Secondary Fine Arts School of China's Central Academy of Fine Arts and University Complutense of Madrid, Spain. Once an art editor, she is now managing her own company, specializing in organizing art and book exhibitions. Her works include *Hua Mulan, the Ancient Chinese Heroine*, first published in the USA and now in English, French, Vietnamese, Chinese and Cambodian; *How to Write Chinese*, published in the USA; *Development of A City*, published in Italy; *Four Great Ancient Inventions*, published in Hong Kong; *Pictorial Chinese History: The Southern Song Dynasty, The Repentant Bird, The One-Headed Woman*, published in Taiwan; and *The Thirty-six Stratagems*, published in China.

Contents

The Magnolia in Blossom   1

Mulan in Disguise   13

Victories on the Battlefield   29

Capturing the Chieftain Alive   75

Declining A Marriage Proposal   97

The Magnolia in Blossom

At the end of China's Eastern Han Dynasty, there was a small beautiful village in Hebei Province called Shangyi Village.

One of the villagers was named Hua Hu.

Hua Hu loved reading and martial arts all his life.

He had ever been a general for credits in war.

Mulan was good at riding. She often acted as general and deployed a group of kids in battle formation on the river bank.

Very soon, Mulan became a "king of the kids" in the village.

CLOG!
CLOG!

At seventeen, Mulan began to learn to do housework.

Mulan in Disguise

Why don't I disguise myself as a man and join the army for father? So long as I am not discovered, I can come back to look after parents in one or two year's time once the war is over. But who knows whether I look like a man or not after wearing man's clothes?

Victories on the Battlefield

Brother Wang, you should know that there's no home without a country.

Others can enjoy family reunion but we can't.

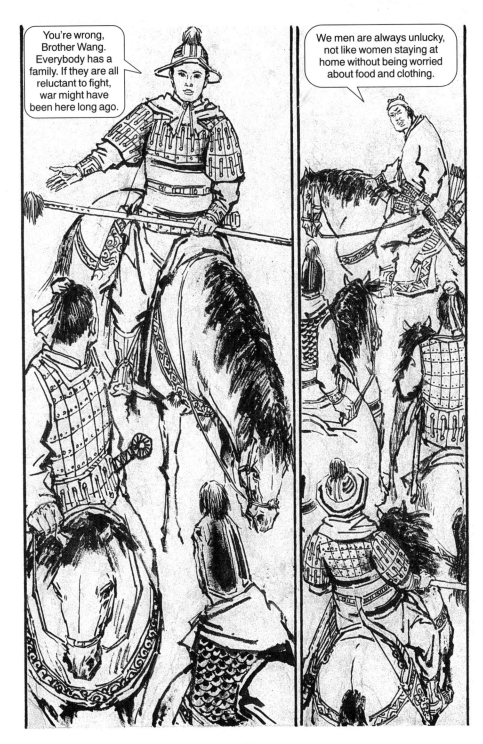

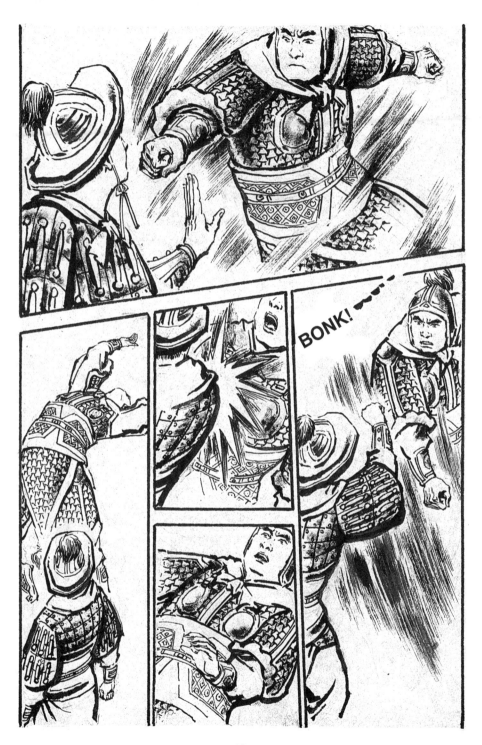

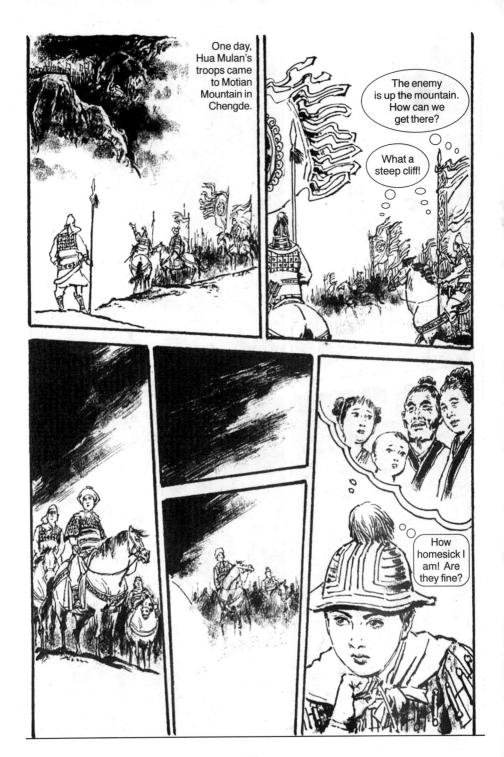

Near Hua Mulan's camp stood a small wineshop run by a mother and her daughter.

Though not addicted to wine, Mulan sometimes dropped in for a rest.

Just as I expected, the enemy is carried away with success.

Busy gathering spoils, the enemy troops failed to be alert.

After the enemy troops fled, Mulan recalled the troops, fearing the emptiness of the city.

Capturing the Chieftain Alive

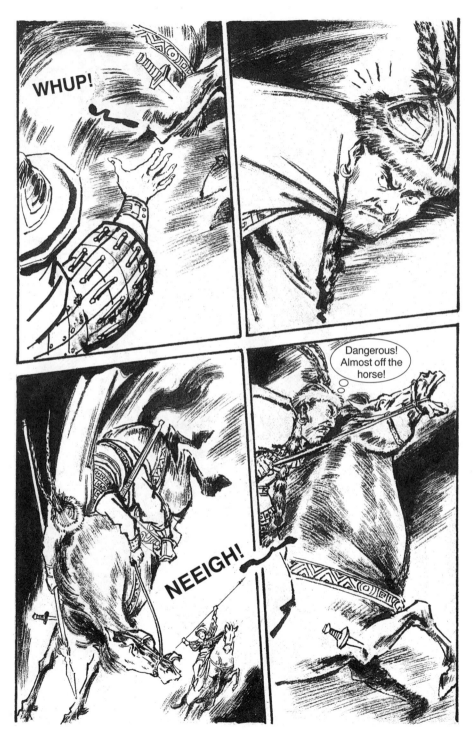

Tu Lizi fought again, fiercely and accurately.

Declining a Marriage Proposal

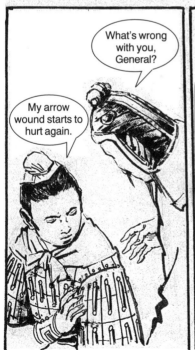

Mulan took off the warrior's robe and put on her long red skirt.

General Hua has become the Huas' daughter again.

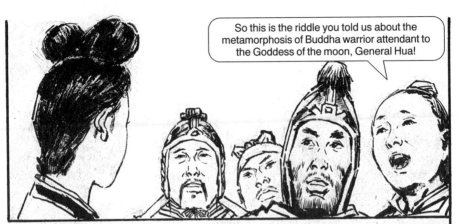

Hilarious Chinese Classics by Tsai Chih Chung

Journey to the West 1 & 2
These books offer more than the all-too-familiar escapades of Tang Sanzang and his animal disciples. Under the creative pen of Tsai Chih Chung, *Journey to the West* still stays its course but takes a new route. En route from ancient China to India to acquire Buddhist scriptures, the Monk and his disciples veer off course frequently to dart into modern times to have fleeting exchanges with characters ranging from Ronald Reagan to Bunny Girls of the Playboy Club.

Romance of the Three Kingdoms
Set in the turbulent Three Kingdoms Period, *Romance of the Three Kingdoms* relates the clever political manoeuvres and brilliant battle strategies used by the ambitious rulers as they fought one another for supremacy.

In this comic version, Tsai Chih Chung has illustrated in an entertaining way the four best-known episodes in the novel.

Madam White Snake
Most of you may be familiar with the story of Madam White Snake. But do you know that Xiaoqing, Madam White Snake's faithful maid, was actually a carp which lived in the waters of the West Lake? Or that Xu Xian was the only boy in a family of eleven children? Or that the self-righteous monk Fa Hai was actually a toad?

Through his lively and entertaining illustrations, Tsai Chih Chung injects much wit and humour into this modern interpretation of the age-old tale.

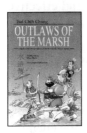

Outlaws of the March
The seven outlaws featured in this comic edition were fugitives in the eyes of the law, but heroes in their own right.

For instance, Tiger Slayer Wu Song killed his adulterous sister-in-law because she had poisoned his brother. And Song Jiang, a clerk in the magistrate's court, was forced to kill his frivolous young wife, to prevent her from exposing his ties with the other outlaws at Liangshan Marsh.

Strategy & Leadership Series by Wang Xuanming

Thirty-six Stratagems: Secret Art of War
Translated by Koh Kok Kiang (cartoons) &
　　　　　　Liu Yi (text of the stratagems)
　A Chinese military classic which emphasizes deceptive schemes to achieve military objectives. It has attracted the attention of military authorities and general readers alike.

Six Strategies for War: The Practice of Effective Leadership
Translated by Alan Chong
　A powerful book for rulers, administrators and leaders, it covers critical areas in management and warfare including: how to recruit talents and manage the state; how to beat the enemy and build an empire; how to lead wisely; and how to manoeuvre brilliantly.

Gems of Chinese Wisdom: Mastering the Art of Leadership
Translated by Leong Weng Kam
　Wise up with this delightful collection of tales and anecdotes on the wisdom of great men and women in Chinese history, including Confucius, Meng Changjun and Gou Jian.

Three Strategies of Huang Shi Gong: The Art of Government
Translated by Alan Chong
　Reputedly one of man's oldest monograph on military strategy, it unmasks the secrets behind brilliant military manoeuvres, clever deployment and control of subordinates, and effective government.

100 Strategies of War: Brilliant Tactics in Action
Translated by Yeo Ai Hoon
　The book captures the essence of extensive military knowledge and practice, and explores the use of psychology in warfare, the importance of building diplomatic relations with the enemy's neighbours, the use of espionage and reconnaissance, etc.

Latest Titles in Strategy & Leadership Series

Chinese Business Strategies

The Chinese are known for being shrewd businessmen able to thrive under the toughest market conditions. The secret of their success lies in 10 time-tested principles of Chinese entrepreneurship.

This book offers readers 30 real-life, ancient case studies with comments on their application in the context of modern business.

Sixteen Strategies of Zhuge Liang

Zhuge Liang, the legendary statesman and military commander during the Three Kingdoms Period, is the epitome of wisdom.

Well-grounded in military principles of Sun Zi and other masters before him, he excelled in applying them in state administration and his own innovations, thus winning many spectacular victories with his uncanny anticipation of enemy moves.

The Adventures of Wisely
(comics series)

1 *The Return of the Hermit*
2 *The Mystery of the Golden Sphere*
3 *Hide-And-Seek*
4 *The Old Cat*
5 *The Sunken Ship*

Love at first sight.

Stormy courtship.

Wisely turns mad...

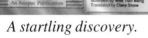

A startling discovery.

Join Wisely and Bai Su as they embark on their perilous adventures!

A 3,000-year-old cat.

亞太圖書有限公司出版

翻譯：王 偉
編著：張德江、美穗
編著：張德江、美穗

花太鼓

《亞太漫畫系列》

RETURN OF THE CONDOR HEROES

神鵰俠侶

Subscription Form

Bestselling martial-art comics by Louis Cha
Illustrated by Wee Tian Beng

Per Issue
Usual: S$8.76
Now: S$7.70
(local order)

Now in 18 volumes, published bimonthly. Subscribe now and enjoy special discounts.

I wish to subscribe for *Return of the Condor Heroes Series* from Volume _____ to Volume _____.

☐ Singapore Order: Nett price of S$7.70 per volume (free postage)
☐ Overseas Order: Nett price of S$10.20 per volume (inclusive of postage by surface mail)
Enclosed is my postal order/money order/cheque/ for S$ _____ (No.: _____)

Name (Mr/Mrs/Ms) _____ Tel _____
Address _____
_____ Fax _____

Please charge the amount of S$ _____ to my VISA/MASTER CARD account (only Visa/Master Card accepted)
Card No. _____ Card Expiry Date _____

Card Holder's Name (Mr/Mrs/Ms) _____ Signature _____

Send to: ASIAPAC BOOKS PTE LTD 996 Bendemeer Road #06-08/09 Kallang Basin Industrial Estate Singapore 339944 Tel: (65)3928455 Fax: (65)3926455
Note: Prices subject to change without prior notice. Each issue to be mailed to you upon publication — one volume every two months.